HOW TO RAISE UP A KID OR TWO

Dedicated to all the parents of the world!
Cheer up! There is a light at the end of the tunnel and it's
not a train coming right at you. They will grow up.
Have patience, drink a little, hide the car keys, and relax.
Follow the instructions in the book exactly and
you will live through it!

HOW TO RAISE UP A KID OR TWO

DR. ANDY KANE

PALADIN PRESS • BOULDER, COLORADO

Other books by Andy Kane:
Care and Feeding of Tenants
No Waiting!: How to Get What You Want, When You Want It
Tenant's Revenge: How to Tame Your Landlord
You're Fired!: How to Turn a Pink Slip into a Golden Opportunity

How to Raise Up a Kid or Two
by Andy Kane

ISBN 1-58160-394-0
Printed in the United States of America

Published by Paladin Press, a division of
Paladin Enterprises, Inc.
Gunbarrel Tech Center
7077 Winchester Circle
Boulder, Colorado 80301 USA
+1.303.443.7250

Direct inquiries and/or orders to the above address.

Illustrations by Steve Soeffing

Visit our Web site at www.paladin-press.com

Table of Contents

Warning

Check with your obstetrician, pediatrician, and a good lawyer before considering any of the advice on the following pages. It is not the intent of the author, publisher, or distributors of this book to encourage behavior that will cause your children to sue you (or worse, us!) at some point in the future. This book is *for entertainment purposes only*!

Preface

The most important part of any book is the preface. It's like an appetizer before a big meal. You get to find out about the author and the when and why about the book. One thing you may notice if you have read any of my previous books is that before my name on this book, it says "Dr." Previous books just said "Andy Kane" as author. I felt that by using the "Dr." prefix with my name, it would give much more credibility to a book on children and since I have a doctor of divinity degree issued by the Universal Life Church in Modesto, California, in 1978, I am entitled to legally use the designation. This degree is similar to that used by the Dr. Martin Luther King, Dr. Norman Vincent Peal, and other notable authors and speakers in the United States of America. I also have considerable funds ($25.00 plus postage) invested in obtaining this degree.

OK, next item ...Why a book on raising kids? Dr. Spock

has a great one if you are looking for a cut-and-dried, medically-oriented manual to produce a couple of cookie-cutter kids. I believe what this world needs is a real-life owner's manual for operating kids! When I purchased my Chevrolet pickup truck, I received a leather-bound, 445-page manual telling me everything I needed to know about the care, operation, and periodic maintenance required for this vehicle. You could almost reconstruct the vehicle using this manual, it's so detailed. It covers every possible event from a flat tire (don't drive on it, change it) to exploding air bags (kid's head may be found in back seat).

This book is the real deal, covers real problems and presents common-sense solutions that are within the reach of every parent. Do these techniques work? I have walking, talking evidence that my solutions work. One piece of evidence is named Colleen, the other is named Glenn. They not alone survived my techniques, but they are well-adjusted, productive members of the community. Ninety-five percent of the stories and suggestions in this book have actually occurred. The other 5 percent are compounds of various events. (That's called artistic license.) Most will probably be considered politically incorrect, but what do you care, as long as your kids make it in the world? If Lee Harvey Oswald's parents had this book, their kid may have turned out fine.

This world is changing rapidly. Many of the new techniques recommended by the professional kid counselors do not work and never will. If you administer punishment today, the kid can call 911 and you will be wearing silver bracelets in an hour. The Boy Scouts are considered a subversive group because they decided to limit their leadership to normal, heterosexual people. Ridiculous! Use the information in this book to bring up these kids and you will have a happy, well-adjusted product.

A manual like this is a necessity. When we brought home our kids from the hospital, we received at discharge a "pamphlet" with some minor information, a couple of free diapers, phlet" with some minor information, a couple of free diapers, and that was it! That pickup truck that came with the detailed manual was probably only kept for 3 or 4 years. We planned on keeping the kids forever and all we got was a two-page, mimeographed pamphlet!

A word of caution. Although the book will be extremely useful for your kid's entire growing up period, you may feel you no longer need it when your kid reaches the adult point. Do not, under any circumstances, give this book to your pregnant sister-in-law! Keep it with your valuable mementos of the kid's childhood. File it with his first report card, distemper shot certificate, bail bond receipts, and work release program discharge, but do not lend or give it to anyone! (I only make money when people buy the book, not borrow it!) Recommend it, but don't lend it.

Read on and God bless America and the First Amendment.

Disclosure Notice

During the time when I was engaged in the planned development of my offspring, I was also active in many other tasks. I was employed by a large manufacturer and I was doing research for several other books. I also had a severe allergy to the smell of dirty diapers and a fondness for the smell of stale beer and cheap perfume. The allergic reaction to a dirty diaper usually caused me to vomit (also known as puke) when I came within an arm's length of a soiled kid.

This reaction required me to limit the actual time spent in the homestead with my smelly little rugrats. Since my time to do the actual training would be extremely limited and I did have the access to a healthy lady (the kid's mom, my lovely wife) who could follow my instructions, a great deal of the hands-on training was accomplished by her. Before the time that the tummy dwellers got loose, I had been successful in training her to assist me in many household and yard tasks.

She proved valuable at these assignments and therefore, I had no qualms about assigning raising-up tasks to her. All in all, she did an excellent job of following my instructions (except for dropping one of the kids on its head!) throughout their formative years. When I decided to write a book on raising up kids, I asked my offspring what they thought of the idea. Their response ranged from "Please, please, *please* don't do it!" To "At least if you do, I will have some evidence to back up the stories no one believes about my childhood!" I asked them what some of their favorite memories were of the raising-up process. They said there were not too many "favorite" memories, but they certainly held many other memories. Some are repeated in this book, but if you run across my kids, don't hold this book against them. They were just innocent bystanders.

Names for Kids

Every kid needs a handle. This moniker is very, very important. Do you remember the old Johnny Cash song "A Boy Named Sue?" There is a lot of merit to the words of this song. The father knew that he was not going to be around when the kid was growing up. He knew being self-sufficient would be a problem growing up without a man around the house. By naming the kid "Sue," he would most certainly learn to fight at an early age. I'm not suggesting naming the kids with girl names for boys or vice versa, but the song does illustrate one important point: the kid has to live with this name his entire life. After you get your jollies introducing your kid by his idiotic name the kid has to go through the rest of his life with the jokes.

My last name is Kane and I could have named my daughter "Candi" (I didn't). I know a family named "Bare" and they named their son, Theodore (Teddy) Bare. A local disc jockey recently named his daughter "Sammy Davis." When you name your kid after a movie star, sports figure, or even a sporting event, you are doing this kid a great disservice. The ridiculous names will cause hundreds of hours of teasing, explaining ("my daddy liked ——") or embarrassment. It most certainly can affect their possibility of success or job advancement. Can you imagine the president of IBM being named "Candi Kane" or the CEO of General Motors being "Teddy Bare?" Tiger Woods is an exception because he chose or was forced into sports, but can you imagine if he had chosen banking or the legal profession? Would you like to trust your life savings with someone named Tiger? How many Rockys do you know? Are any of them not Italian? It's a favorite name for fathers to hang on the new baby to ensure that when he grows up, he will be tough. What if he decides to become a flute player with the philharmonic instead of a boxer? Keep in mind that after you get your fun, this kid has to live with the name.

Another thing that will cause kids with unusual names big problems is that they will be in the 8th grade before they can spell their own names. I was lucky. Andy Kane only has eight letters and I could spell and write my name when I was three years old.

Many parents want to honor themselves by naming the kid after themselves (George Foreman named all his kids—sons *and* daughters—George Foreman!) and this can cause many problems for both parents and offspring. Let's say your name is George Bush and you live in Kenybuckport, Maine. You name your son, George Bush. He grows up and gets a drunk-driving ticket. The name may appear in the Kenybuckport paper and George Sr.'s friends may read this and assume that he is hitting the bottle. It may also happen in reverse. A father may be arrested or charged with a heinous crime (rape, sodomy, or robbery) and since the name is the same, the son may be confused as the perpetrator. Another problem is when a Junior is created, this "Junior" nickname will follow this person until he croaks. What do you imagine when you hear the name, Junior? I bet you visualize a kid about 5 years old, in short pants, a lollypop in his mouth, holding an adult's hand. I know many Juniors who are in their 70s, 80s, and older and the Junior name hardly fits the real person. You should also avoid using a name that will be replaced by a nickname if the nickname could be considered offensive, such as Richard (Dick) or Victor David (V.D.).

Think ahead before the kid is born, sit down and pick a name for a boy and a girl. Consider implication and complication. Say the name over and over with the last name. I know a woman who wanted all her kid's initials to be "W.W." Her last name was Wilson. She named her little girl Wendy. Her next kid was a boy and was named Wayne. Another boy comes along and she devised a name based upon the standard name of Robert, but she named him "Wabert!" Every time the kid told someone his name, they thought he was tongue-tied! They assumed he was trying to say "Robert."

It is not wise to saddle a kid with an unusual name. I think that a parent who gives a kid an idiot name or even calls him by a nickname that sticks with him should be charged with child abuse. My brother called one of his kids "Stinky." I assume it has something to do with his pre-toilet training time, but the name stuck with him for a long time. Can you imagine him at school? "Hey Stinky, are you going to the prom?" Use you head when assigning a name. You should also consider the length of the name. The kid will have to sign his name hundreds of thousands of times over his lifetime. If his name is l-o-n-g, it will take additional time every time he signs it. If you have decided on "John" for a name, why not eliminate the silent "H" and just use Jon! Richard will also be called Rick. Why not just name him "Rick"?! The easier a kid's name is to pronounce, spell or remember will make his life that much easier. I knew a guy once who's name was Zigfried H. Henninsdorpher. What a monicker! When it comes to names, remember "KISS" (Keep it simple, stupid)!

Parental Qualifications

Many years ago, I would have listed

1. Responsible adults
2. Happily married
3. Stable home environment
4. Financially secure

Today, to have a child, it just takes a working vagina. Husbands are optional. A lover, passerby, or sperm donor will suffice. There is no training required.

You remember in the beginning I mentioned my Chevrolet pickup truck? The one with the 445-page, leather-bound instruction manual? Before I could legally use this vehicle, I was required to obtain a driver's license and go through the associated training to take the test. I also had to register the vehicle and prove financial responsibility. After I accomplished this, I was able to drive it.

If you want to have a kid, just get knocked up. It's as simple as that. It's so simple that many don't even know they are going to be a parent until months later!

Recently, in Rochester, New York, a parent sat through a murder trial of his third son. The son was convicted and sent to prison. The father was interviewed after the trial by several reporters and it was discovered that he had three sons—the other two were already in prison for other murders! Three out of three, all for different murders. He indicated that he, as a parent, knew exactly what the cause of this problem was. The problem was the availability of guns! Keep in mind, this is a parent speaking. I believe he should go back and take "Parenting 101" over again. He actually believed that the gun was responsible, not his kids!

The simple thing is, there are really no legal requirements for being a parent. Any moron can and will do it. One thing I have noticed is that when some misfit has a kid and she is in the hospital, her friends, parents, and acquaintances all show up with flowers, candy, and presents. She is queen for a day. Until she had the little bundle of joy, she was a nothing. Now, she is the center of attention. Even the nurses, who she does not even know, are fussing all over her. In a few days, she is discharged and returns to her hovel with the stuffed toys, candy, and dead flowers. Maybe one or two people come to see little Herman. They come once or twice, but don't return because of the dirty diaper smell and because she sits there watching soap operas all day. After a few weeks of despair, she remembers the fuss that was made over her when she was queen for a day. You guessed it—she gets pregnant again so she can revisit the maternity ward and get a little attention.

There are some simple tests to decide if you should consider being a parent:

- Add up all the teeth in your and your mate's immediate families. If the total is less than 25, forget it.
- Did anyone in your family graduate from high school,

grammar school, nursery school? Add up the total of highest grades and if it is less than 10, forget it.

- If you don't have a job that pays more than minimum wage, if you do not work more than 25 hours a week, or if you say, "Do you want fries with that?", forget it.
- If you don't have a permanent address or if you have moved more than 12 times in the last six months, forget it.
- If you are on a first-name basis with the local mental health clinic workers or police department, forget it.
- If your mate also has the same last name or you met your mate at the family picnic, forget it.
- If your sister, brother or other immediate family have produced "unusual" kids (twins attached at the hip, extremely large heads, missing parts, or extra parts), forget it.
- If the last several pets you had died of any "unusual" cause (starvation, mutilation, amputation), forget it.
- If the last several pets you had ran away, forget it.
- If your mother had the same last name as your father before they were married and *they* met at the family picnic, forget it.
- If you don't like kids, forget it.
- If you have accidentally lost any live things (like pets, small brother or sister, kids you were watching for the neighbors), forget it.
- If you already have a kid or several kids and you do not know their names, forget it.
- If you already have a kid or several kids and you have not seen them in several days, but you know they must be around some place because the junk food is being consumed by someone or something, forget it.

These are some of the guide lines I suggest, but i'm sure you get the general idea. A kid should have an even chance if you bring one into this world. Think it over before you diddle.

Womb Dwellers

When the kid is still in the womb he is nice and happy and has everything he needs—food, warmth, dark so he can catch some shut-eye. He's carried around so he does not have to exert himself, no worries. This is the ideal time for parents, also. No crying, screaming, diaper deals, formula, spitting up. This will probably be the only time the kid is quiet and does not cause trouble for the next 20 or 30 years. Enjoy it—savor every minute of his imprisonment.

During this period, medical experts suggest that the mother not drink booze, smoke or chew tobacco, use dope, or other stupid things. It's also suggested that wild sex be avoided near the end so the kid does not get a hole poked in its head. It is, however, permissible for the daddy to do most all of the above in any amount he sees fit. There may be some reasoning for abstinence for the owner of the womb, but

these policies are only a decade or so old. That means that about 80 percent of the people now walking around the USA are the product of mothers who never heard of these restrictions. That's a lot of healthy, normal people whose time in the womb was during the time mothers were socializing (drinking and smoking and whatever else) and these people have ended up no worse for the experience.

I am sure my mother smoked and drank while I was hibernating in her stomach. I have never smoked any type of cigarette in my life. I never even had "I didn't inhale" type of experience. I would, therefore, assume that a mother smoking does not necessarily mean the kid will be a puffer. My mother's drinking did not make me an alcoholic. I've had a few drinks in my day. I believe that at one time I probably kept a few brewery workers busy, but I certainly was not an alcoholic. When I decided to stop my drinking several years ago, it was an easy step. I just stopped cold turkey with no ill effects.

Now drugs are a different story. Many babies are born addicted to drugs and there is evidence of that. I would suggest a couple of drinks, maybe a cigarette or two, but no drugs while that little guy is in the womb. It's best to keep the kid reasonably healthy while he's in your belly, because if he is addicted or unhealthy after he escapes from the womb, it will be a big, big problem. In some areas you can even be arrested for kid abuse if your offspring tests positive for drugs at birth. Don't take chances.

If this is your first kid, you may be inclined to feed it table scraps or pizza. That won't work yet. When they are little (and most newborns are), they prefer milk or a reasonable facsimile. Mother's milk is best and they say it wards off certain illnesses and it also tastes good (I know, mmm, mmm!). I am not a nutritionist, so the food category is not a big thing for me. I have reached some conclusions through observations.

The more a kid eats, the bigger he gets. If your goal is to create a linebacker, chuck him full of goodies. If you want a jockey, feed him sparsely. This is a part when you have to use your head a little. Since the little ones seldom have choppers, some foods like peanuts, steak, and corn on the cob should be avoided. There is an isle in the grocery store marked "baby grub." Almost everything in this isle will fit in the kid's mouth. Use caution. Some of these items will produce diapers that require the service of a hazardous waste team!

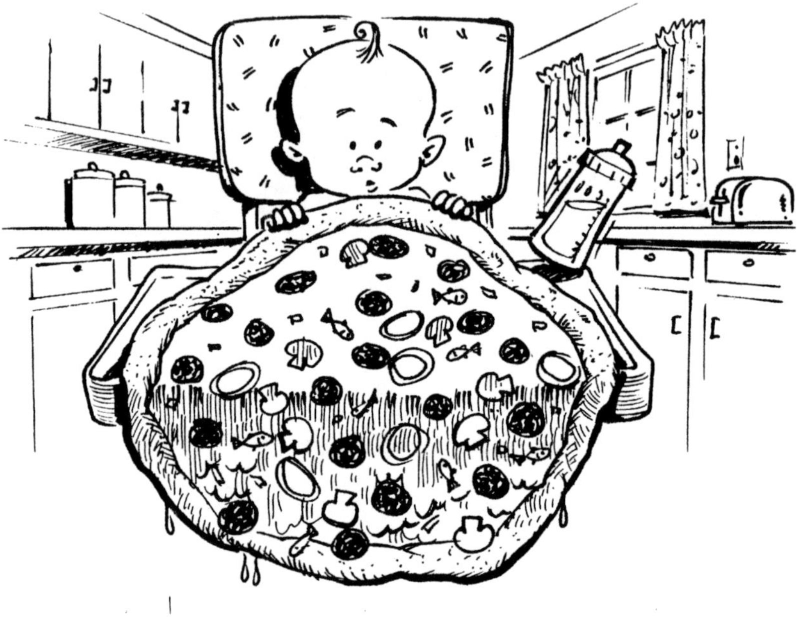

As the kid goes from the "just hatched" stage to walking around and biting the other objects in the house, he's ready for pizza and other tasty grown-up dishes. I find it hard to believe that kids should only eat specific foods and food groups to grow up strong.

One of the things that separate humans from the animal race is our ability to use eating utensils. I believe it is very important and healthier to wean kids off using their hands to stuff the chow in the mouth and into proper use of the knife and fork. These kids will be judged on their table manners by their friends, employers, and others. We gave them a good easy name in a previous chapter, now let's put some manners to work and help them to appear as quality kids and young adults.

I have seen some pretty nice chicks eat like they were from a refugee camp and if they did not chow down in two minutes, someone was going to grab their supper. Obviously, my opinion of them changed. When I first saw them, I considered making them my queen. After I saw their table manners, I would not even consider them qualified to walk my dog.

I personally have a limited selection of foods that I consume. I try to balance my diet to 50 percent of what I know is good for health and 50 percent that I know is bad. It works. Try and get the kids started out eating right and they probably will continue eating right through life. If you do not know what is good and what is not, try the Internet or good health books for some advice. I am a landlord and over the years, I have seen my tenants' kids eating everything from cat food, raw hamburger, or fishing bait. They all survived and appear to be in good, physical condition. You will also notice that young kids will and do eat just about anything that they can get in their mouth. Some will not hurt them (worms, bugs with the exception of bees) but some are not good (pennies, small toys, screws, nails) and are hard to digest. You should try to keep the latter items out of the kids' reach from birth until at least age 19.

Eat up and enjoy life!

Safety

As soon as you bring the new one home, you will probably start putting "safety covers" on all your wall outlets. This is done so that when the kid starts crawling, he can not stick a fork in the wall outlet.

This is ridiculous! By childproofing all the electric outlets, you have eliminated a learning experience for the kid. If he ever gets out of your house and stays at grandma's, he will then stick the fork in her outlet and probably also give grandma heart failure. My suggestion is not to childproof anything! A little shock will not kill the brat, unless he is standing in a puddle of water; 110 volts is a minor amount of voltage and it will be a good learning experience.

An eye surgeon once told me an important fact about little bitty babies. Parents are always afraid the kid will put something in his eye. The surgeon told me that every single baby does put something in his eye. They stick their fingers

in their eyes. Every baby does it once and by that lesson, they immediately learn never to do it again. You will never see a kid poke himself in the eye twice. That firsthand experience lasts a lifetime!

I have carried a gun for 30 years. It is a .25 caliber automatic. If I were to listen to all the gun safety gurus, I would unload this gun each time I entered my castle. I would put a trigger lock on the trigger and put the gun in a drawer in the bedroom and lock the drawer. I would put the bullets in a locked metal box and that box would be in a locked drawer in the den. I would then put the keys for the trigger lock, two drawers, and the metal box in a safe hiding place. This is the approved way indicated by the safety nuts. If I did this and an armed intruder kicked in my door, I would have to run and find the keys, unlock the two drawers, the trigger, the metal bullet box and reinstall the clip! I assume that the intruder would give me a sporting chance to accomplish these tasks. Lots of luck! I would have been shot, my wife raped and the kids assaulted, and my money gone.

Since I realize all these safety things were insane, I never did any of the above. I simply showed the kids the loaded gun on my nightstand, carefully explained the use, the danger, and that this gun or any gun they found anywhere, anytime, should never be touched. Guess what? Both kids are still alive. This is the intelligent way to teach kids safety. If you do the crazy gun lock-up procedure, it will actually challenge the kids to find the keys, the bullets, and the gun. It's like a game. Hiding the gun does not teach kids respect for guns. If an untrained kid sees a gun in a lot or at a playmate's house, he will be inclined to inspect or shoot it, since he has not been taught gun safety, just gun hiding. A gun is an object. It can't do anything without human help. Common sense should tell you that concentrating your effort on the human aspect is the only way to prevent disasters.

When the Columbine shooting took place, there was an immediate call for more gun laws! There are presently more than 22,000 gun laws on the books in the United States! When the kids brought the guns to school they broke hundreds of laws and one commandment: Thou shalt not kill. Forget about the object and concentrate on the human.

Throughout the house, there are many dangers and if you eliminate them with safety devices, the one time you forget to lock the gate on the stairs, the double latch on the lower kitchen counter cabinet, the pot of water on the stove, the kid will be injured. He will yank the pot over, take a header down the stairs, or drink drain cleaner.

Teach the kid to be aware of these dangers and not to do the life-threatening things. Then he will be safe everywhere, even at grandma's, where all the safety devices have not been installed!

But I would not test a kid by leaving dangerous items on lower shelves or where they can reach them. Use common sense and place them out of reach. Especially watch pills and other pretty medicines. They are colorful and may attract the brats. If you take pills, do not take them in the kids' presence.

Go in the bathroom and close the door when you pop your pills. Remember, "monkey see, monkey do." A good thing to do is have syrup of ipecac handy and the number of the local poison control office posted near the phone. If you have a cigarette lighter, you should also show and explain the lighter to the kid as you did with the gun. Teach them to respect the lighter and never to touch it. If you notice any sparkle in his eyes while you are explaining the danger of a lighter and fire, raise the insurance coverage on your dwelling.

Keeping the kids out of the road is also a good idea. It's hard to get them to realize that a car is a danger to them. They see you washing and waxing the car, they ride in the car and listen to nice music. They consider the car a friendly item. How do you show them that the car is a dangerous item? The next time you are driving and the kid is with you and you see some road kill, stop and examine it. Get out and closely

observe the flat squirrel or skunk. (Even better, if you come upon an accident scene and can show the little one a flat kid.)

Show kids that the nice car can kill you in one second. Explain that although cars have brakes and can sometimes stop before it hits them, a lot depends on the driver. For a car to stop, several things are important:

- The driver must see the kid in time to mash the brake pedal.
- If the driver is talking or on a cell phone, drinking, or eating a Big Mac, they may be distracted and not see the kid until he hears the big bang.
- Kids are small and hard to see.

If you teach your kids to stay away from the road , they will be reasonably safe. Then they are about 10 or 12, teach them to look both ways before crossing and be sure nothing is coming.

I'm going to mention another hazard: water. Kids will never drown if you keep them away from the water. I had an unusual situation as my kids were growing up. I lived at a resort type area. In front of my house was one of the largest of the Great Lakes. In back of my house was the highway. I could have done what many other neighbors did and put a fence up all around my house (at great expense) and turn my nice home in a resort area to a concentration camp. This is the moron's solution to most problems. (Having a fence is another bad idea. The kid will watch for you to forget to close the gate and escape into the danger of the lake or highway.) The best idea is to train the kid to the dangers of the road and water. My kids were shown and told of the dangers and never ran in the road or fell in the lake.

When you teach kids to observe dangers and play safe at a young age, they will be safe throughout life.

Baby Talk

I have often wondered what a baby thinks when he's in the crib and several adults are talking to each other in plain, everyday English and then they approach the crib, smile, and start talking some unusual language. (Hoow izz dee itty biddy baybee?!) I think this must confuse the kid to no end. Here he is, trying to learn to communicate with the huge people around him, he has a brain about the size of a grape, and these people want him to learn two languages. It will be a lot easier for the kid if he can just master one language. Use the same tone of voice you would if you were talking to your parole officer or a friend when you talk to the little one. Use the same words. It's a lot easier for a kid to understand and the sooner you get the kid to understand commands, the sooner you can train them. Refer to the bathroom as guess what? The bathroom, not the potty. Call dogs, dogs, not bow wow's. Call cats, cats, not kitty cats. And don't pinch 'em on the cheek every time you talk to them!

Babysitters/ Temporary Guards

There will always be a time when you have to leave the kid with someone for some reason. This can be a traumatic experience for you, the kid, and the sitter. Your pride and joy will be with a stranger? You should do some research before selecting a sitter. Incidentally, have you ever wondered where the word "sitter" comes from? Do they sit on the kid?

Set up some requirements and qualifications for the sitter you are going to entrust your flesh and blood with. Will they work for lower wages than a worker in Kathie Lee's sweat shop? Can they use a phone and speak English? Will they still be there when you return? These are important considerations.

If she is decent looking or over the age of 12, will she have time to check on the kid while she entertains her boyfriend?

Some of your first choices for kid control are:

- Your parents. How did they treat you when you were a kid? Have the scars healed? Are you able to talk without stuttering? What will they charge?
- Friends of yours that like kids. Are they sober, off drugs, or in withdrawal? What will they charge?
- Friends who have children the same age. Do they still like kids? What will they charge?
- Nursery school. Are they licensed? Is their license revoked? When will they get it back? How many kids? (A good formula is that the number of kids divided by number of attendants gives you a rough idea of how much time they will spend with your kid. Example: 42 kids and two attendants means each attendant is watching 21 kids!) How much will they charge?
- Strangers from the neighborhood. Get some I.D. Have they ever taken care of a kid, pet, or themselves? How much will they charge?

Evaluate them all and go with the cheapest.

I once hired a girl to watch my kids. When I returned, the kids told me that if they cried or made trouble, the sitter held them over an open staircase and said if they did not shape up, she would drop them! That initially disturbed me that she did this, but after I thought about it, she didn't really drop them and they did shape up. Maybe she had a good idea. I hired her again.

Be sure to leave phone numbers so that sitter can contact you if she gets a better offer while you are gone and has to jump ship. While I was growing up, I had very few sitters. We had an old maid aunt who was a retired teacher and she was readily available. My brother and I dreaded the arrival of the extremely heavy, bearded, smelly lady. We were well behaved and spent as much time in our room as humanly possible. If you have anything like this available, you may give it a try.

Clothing

Have you ever noticed the National Geographic specials on TV? You see little kids, barefoot and with a loincloth, running, climbing trees, killing goats, and having an all around nice time. They look about as happy as a kid can be.

Next time you are in the mall, look around at the kids dressed in designer pants and brand name sneakers. You will notice they don't even look happy! Most don't even know they have designer clothing because they are not old enough to read the labels. It costs more for one outfit of designer clothing than the National Geographic kid will ever see in his lifetime!

I'm not suggesting loincloths for the kids, but Wal-Mart has practical, economical clothing for all ages. It's idiotic to spend big bucks on sneakers for a baby who does not walk and will outgrow them before he takes his first step. Many kids wear hand-me-downs from other kids in the same family or neighborhood and they live through it. I know one successful businessman who always knew what he would be wearing next year because his older brother was wearing it this year. It never bothered him to wear hand-me-downs and he became successful.

Use the designer clothing money for something else that will benefit the kid later, like investing in a stock portfolio for his college education or bail money.

Vacations

After you have a kid or two, you will realize that vacations are not optional, they are required. Even one kid can drive you nuts if you don't get a little break once in a while.

Have you ever considered doing away with the little one? That's when you know you need a vacation. Vacations need not be long trips or two-week cruises. If you save your bucks all year for a big splash, you are doing a disservice to yourself. One vacation is not enough to keep your sanity. Instead of one big, expensive trip, take 10 or 12 weekend jaunts. It's healthier and probably costs the same as the big one. There are two kinds of vacations. There is the real vacation, when you leave the kids behind, and there is the vacation where it is just a change of scenery. The kids go on the second one.

Let's analyze the real vacation first. This is you and your spouse or significant other and a romantic getaway. It can

range from just a weekend at Sunny Buns Clothing-Optional Resort to a 10-day cruise, but it should be just the two of you, no kids. I even suggest that you erase the offspring from your mind. Take their pictures out of your wallet. Don't call, even once. Don't mention them to anyone you meet. Leave a number where they can call in emergency only.

My wife was always reluctant to leave all traces of the kids at home because she "missed them." A solution to the "missed them" problem is to bring an emergency kit. Bring a small tape recorder of them screaming. Put a dirty diaper in a plastic bag. If the "missed them" hits, play the tape and unzip the bag and take a whiff! This is a guaranteed cure.

If more parents used the real vacation procedure, I believe there would be fewer children flung off seven-story buildings. (Remember, children can not fly!) One important part of the real vacation I almost forgot. Never leave the kids home alone. Never, no matter how old they are. You say they are 14, 17, 18, and 21! I repeat never leave the kids home alone. The older they are, the more danger. Party, drinking, sex, robbery, fire, explosives, pregnancy. All are consequences of leaving the kids alone. I usually had at least a drop-in person to make unexpected checks on the residence if I was away for more than a few hours. I had a good friend who was a cop. I gave him a key and told him if he found anyone except my kids in the home to arrest them. It worked well.

The second kind of vacation is good, but not quite as relaxing. You take the brood to Wally World and ride everything in sight twice. The kids (and you) get completely exhausted and ask if it's all right to go to bed at 5:30 p.m. This vacation, due to the dragging the kids factor, should seldom be done, maybe once per year.

I took my kids on an annual vacation and they had a great time. I picked the destination and they ranged from a beauty contest in Canada to the Daytona 500. They even got to see a riot firsthand (I actually started it by bringing a band back to the resort after they stopped playing at a local joint). They saw the arrival of the National Guard and the use of fire hoses to control drunken partygoers celebrating the Fourth of July. I believe that my kids have many memorable vacations to discuss with their children. Not many kids have their vacations mentioned on the national news (I recount the riot years later, because I'm sure the statute of limitations has expired!).

Plan your vacations wisely and in advance. The reason you plan in advance is so you have a carrot on a stick. As you are dealing with an unruly child, you can look forward to playing the slots at the Indian casino next week. It helps relax you. Getting back to the thoughts of offing your kid. Many states have recently passed laws that allows you to, instead of shooting them and depositing them in the dumpster at the 7-11, legally drop them off at a police station, fire house, or government building. They must be alive at time of drop off. I'm not sure of the age limits on the kids disposal process, but I'm sure you could contact the local child abuse group.

Remember, vacations are not a luxury. They are a requirement for good mental health—yours and the kids. Don't go to the same place every time. Pick a different destination to add some variety to life. I also do not recommend travel agencies. They tend to produce septic vacations where everything is planned. That's too much like a job. Make your own plans to fit your needs. If you like sports, plan a Super Bowl vacation or Olympics. You might even like a "do nothing" vacation where you take a six pack and a big towel and lay on the beach all day. The most important part of raisin' up kids is the time away from them. Use it wisely.

Chapter Sequence/ Weird Kids

Unlike many other books that follow the kid from birth to 18 years old, chapter by chapter, in chronological order, this book does not. The reason may be due to anything from my heavy drinking for 50 years to the fact that events such as vacations, schooling, food, and tattoos seldom follow in the order in which books are laid out.

There is an index that will direct you to the right chapter. Use it. I threw this in here because you may expect some logical sequence to this book and that will not be the case.

Weird kids ... This book is also written using the premise that your kid or kids are reasonably normal and have all their parts and the parts are in the right places. From time to time, kids do arrive with deformities—an extra ear, two left hands, etc. If UPS were delivering them, you would not sign for them. Many of these kids grow up to be productive and I am not putting them down. It's just that my experience is with regular-issue type brats. If you have a kid that is irregular, I am sure there is a group (Society for the Prevention of Cruelty to Kids with Three Ears) or organization devoted to assisting your offspring. I have never heard of a deformity that did not have an organization to assist the parents. They usually have funding or programs for assisting in raising up these kids. Ask the social worker at that hospital and I am sure you will be referred to the appropriate group. Believe me, every possible disease, affliction or defect has a group. They are well founded and usually can assist you.

PUNISHMENT

- Brass knuckles
- Electric chair
- Lethal injection
- Cattle prod
- Thumb screws
- Stun gun
- Dungeon
- Cat-o-nine-tails
- Straight jacket
- Leather belt
- Wooden spoon
- Solitary confinement
- Shunning
- Starvation
- Pit bulls
- Gallows

I'm not actually suggesting the above, just mentioning some of the punishments used in our society. It might be fun to have some of the items around the house to put a scare in the little ones.

A gallows in the back yard could serve as a swing when the kids were behaving well but if they misbehaved...

An electric chair could make a nice piece of porch furniture but if they misbehaved...

A dungeon in the basement, equipped with spiders and cobwebs could serve as a fruit cellar but if they misbehaved... I think you get the idea.

Many times the threat of punishment is a greater deterrent than the actual punishment. My mother was limited to the punishments available to her during my raisin' up period, 50 years ago. She could not deprive me of TV because it had not been invented, yet. She could not give me "time-out" because that phrase had not yet been coined. Her punishments were simple. For a minor offense (missed homework, didn't clean room) there was "the belt." It was always hanging behind the kitchen door where we could see it. The next step was punishment for major offenses (fighting with sibling, not taking out the trash, skipping school). My mother, being from a good Irish family, used a variation of the dungeon punishment.

We had a well-stocked fruit cellar. A cold, damp, fruit cellar. A couple of spiders were also inhabiting this area. For major offenses, we were assigned time in the fruit cellar. Due to the number of offenses that got me dungeon time during my youth, I am proficient at reciting the ingredients of nearly every fruit or vegetable that comes in a can. When I was only half bad, my time in the fruit cellar was with the light on. Of course, when we were assigned time in the fruit cellar, we could not bring comics or books to pass the time, so reading cans of fruits or vegetables helped pass the time.

When we did something that required severe punishment, some dastardly deed, the fruit cellar time was without the luxury of light. In the dark, anything that you felt against

your skin would be considered a tarantula! Needless to say, I tried my best to avoid dastardly deeds.

Today's parents have many punishments that will not leave lasting scars (remember, brass knuckles, stun gun, cattle prod, cat-o-nine-tails, and pit bulls leave marks that the child abuse workers can use against you). The one most used and is completely useless is, "Wait until your father gets home!" This idiotic threat does two things. It teaches the kid that the mother is afraid of the brat, otherwise, she would dole out the punishment herself and it gives the kid time to get away at 5:30 p.m. when daddy comes home. Another stupid trick is, "You're going to bed without supper." These kids are American, overweight, and their last meal was probably enough to feed a family of four in a third world country for a week. The kid gets some extra sleep and you won't even hear his belly growl.

Kids today have events that may be taken away from them, such as parties, sports, or after-school activities. You can confiscate their cell phones, deprive them of TV or computer access. I would make the punishment fit the crime. One night of no TV, solitary confinement to his or her room, and no phone are a good sentence for minor infractions. Multiple nights of the same for major infractions. You can add work to the sentences (cut the grass, wash the windows, or clean the basement) if they don't get the idea after a few nights of confinement.

For drastic deeds, add loss of allowance or monetary fine ($5 or $10) that has to be paid to you. Keeping kids in line gets harder as they grow. Just yelling at a two-year-old usually does the trick, but as they get older the punishment must be stiffer. Remember the old saying, "Spare the rod, spoil the child." Laws today may reduce the frequency of using a rod, but the meaning of the slogan is still true.

Training a kid is like training a dog. It must be done from the beginning or it will be next to impossible. How many people do you know that let their dog jump on people? I'll bet their kids are untrained, also. If you have to whack a kid once in a while, a rolled up newspaper like you use on a dog will also work on the kid's posterior. It takes a little time to train a kid, but it will be worth it. Don't you wish that the hillside strangler and Jeffrey Dahmer's parents had spent a little more time training their kids?

A friend of mine had an novel idea regarding kids' punishment. It was convoluted, but very interesting. From the time his kids were little, he reversed the punishment/reward procedure. If the kids were bad, he gave them treats, ice cream, candy, or a forced trip to the mall where they had to walk around for at least an hour. When they were good, he let them clean the garage or house, paint the porch, rake leaves, or other household chores. Since they associated the normal good things as punishment they seldom wanted those things and since they were good at a larger rate than bad, a lot of things got done around the house. Strange, but true!

Adopted or Turkey-Baster Kids

Many times the father's or mother's plumbing is not working and therefore, the joy of producing a little one is denied. They will try all sorts of remedies—from a witch doctor, chiropractor, or voodoo artist to standing on their heads during intercourse or visiting Internet chat rooms. If the plumbing problem is isolated to the male, they may resort to the turkey baster route. This is done using sperm from who knows where and injecting it into the woman.

It works and I know a couple of ladies who used this procedure to a certain degree of satisfaction, but there are problems. There is no guarantee that the sperm in the fruit jar actually came from Lance Perfect III, whose resumé indicated an IQ equal to Einstein's and included a photo that looked like an ad for the latest body building equipment info-mercial.

If you give this a try, I would suggest a face-to-face meeting, a background check with the police, and a secure chain to ensure the sperm travels from the donor to the turkey baster. You probably have seen movies based upon a mass murderer donating the seed for little mass murderers. It's artistic license by the director of the movie, but it certainly is a possibility. Many ladies use this technique to have children without the hassle of using a real-life guy. Since they are desperate for a little one, they are excellent candidates for fraud or bait-and-switch schemes. If you are of this persuasion, be extra careful.

I would also avoid the attorneys that offer surrogate moms or adoption outside of regular channels. Especially avoid the foreign country adoption. You could be killed or held for ransom when you go to pick up your purchase. You may encounter last-minute bribes and threats. You may never return. If you pay for a mother's expenses during her fat time, she may back out after the kid is out of the womb and there is nothing you can do to get your bucks back. Even worse, she

may give you the kid and then take it back in a few weeks after you have come to like it.

The papers are full of scams perpetrated by attorneys who skirt the law, but avoid arrest due to technologies. I would almost say that if you and someone else cannot produce an offspring by the normal methods or with minor medical assistance, consider a dog instead. There are many advantages to having a dog instead of a kid:

- Dogs are housebroken in just eight weeks.
- Pedigree papers are certified.
- You don't need a second phone line for a dog.
- Dogs never bug you to get a kid.
- If your dog is bad, it can't be blamed on your genes.
- Even if you whack your dog with a newspaper in the morning, he will be at the door with his tail wagging tonight.
- You'll never get peanut butter and jelly on your computer keyboard from your dog.

- You can teach a dog to bring the paper in when he is just six months old.
- Dogs don't run up huge 900-number sex-line bills.
- Average cost of sending a dog to school is $100, a kid costs $125,000 plus.
- Dogs don't outgrow their coats.
- Dogs don't raid your liquor cabinets.

If you decide on a kid, either adopted, turkey baster, or regular issue, just remember: I warned you!

Moving

Being in the real estate business for a long time, I have encountered many families who did not want to move "until the kids graduate." These parents declined job offers and transfers to better climate, just so their kids would not have to make new friends. They thought they were sacrificing their lives and jobs to help the kids. They were actually hurting the kids by staying in the same location where they would not have to make new friends.

Having friends and acquaintances are an important factor of a kid's life and no matter what business occupation or trade the kid eventually gets into, the number of friends and acquaintances will determine his success or how easy his life will be. Do you think that the CEO of the Ajax Widgit company got that job just because he has superior knowledge of Widgit? No, he had friends on the board.

I am in the business of selling houses, businesses, and

investment property and if I didn't have thousands of friends, I would not be successful. If you deprive a kid of making new childhood friends, you limit him to the 125 kids at his school. If you move, he keeps the 125 friends he made at the first school and gains 125 friends at the second school. If you move again, he makes 125 more friends at the third school and by the time he gets to the eighth grade, he now has 375 friends! He is 250 friends ahead of the kid that stayed at one school. Maybe some of these new friends will be on the board of Ajax Widget company in 20 years and make your kid CEO!

The more friends the kid makes, the better his skill at making friends becomes. The kid shouldn't just concentrate on making friends with the nice upper-crust type kids, he should become friends with every type of kid, short of the out-and-out criminal types. Even if the people who occupy a unit at your new location have six kids who are proven to be lowlifes due to heredity, your kid should add them to his list of friends.

Some day in later life, one of these misfits may be necessary to pump his septic tank, clean his estate, paint his house, or do some other job that misfits gravitate to. Having one of these creatures as a friend or acquaintance will save him bucks and/or get his job done better. I would say that I have several thousand friends or acquaintances throughout the country. Probably one third would be considered influential. (One is a billionaire, many are millionaires.) One third are average Joe's, one third are misfits, drunks or criminals. Most I met at an early age and all have proved useful in my life. The more friends of all types your kid acquires, the greater his chances at success will be! Teach them to be polite and friendly and this will almost assure success. Moving is good for kids ... Keep moving!

Telephones

I'm talking now about the phone in your abode, the one you and your spouse rely on to communicate with the outside world. Kids consider this an amusement device. If they give the number to their friends, you will be walking to the nearest pay phone to call your bet in. There are two methods of retaining some use of your household phone. The first is to scrape the little decal with your number on it off the phone before your kid gets the number. Memorize the number first and be sure it is unlisted so the kid can't get it from the information operator. You also forbid the kid, under pain of death, to ever touch the phone.

This may work for awhile. The second method is to have a children's line installed. This may help, but it also teaches the kid to use the phone. You should immediately block all 900-line calls from every line in the house. If you want to call the 900 sex lines, you can do it from your job!

In addition to the hard-wired phone, the kids will insist they are the only ones in the entire school that do not have their own cell phones! You can tell them that by not having their own cell phone, they will stand out, or that they will make a lot of new friends (Can I use your phone?), or that the microwaves that are emitted from this device can cause brain damage and if they have a brain, you don't want it damaged further.

If they eventually get a job at the burger palace, they can then get a cell phone and pay their own bill. This will teach them responsibility. Tell them you know a famous realtor in upstate New York who has never owned or talked on a cell phone and has done quite well without it. Habitual use of a cell phone will distract you as a driver and also consume an enormous amount of your free time. It is estimated that less than 1/100 of one percent of cell phone talk is of urgent nature. That means that 99 and 99/100 percent of cell phone talk is just pure bullshit.

Toys

Toys and games are very popular with kids. Many parents express their love (or lack of) by showering kids with toys. This is especially true of parents who grew up with very little. They want to be sure that every child of theirs has every toy available, especially at Christmas time.

I actually feel sorry for a little kid with a brain the size of a grape or in some cases, the size of a raisin. He opens 65 presents on Christmas morning and is overwhelmed mentally by the volume. He can only play with one thing at a time. He has a very, very short attention span and is now confronted with a room full of toys.

I never had this problem and I am thankful to my parents that I did not. I received one toy for Christmas each year unless it was a big ticket item. If it was an expensive item, I only received half a present. My brother got the other half.

(We shared the electric train and the phonograph.) Since we only received one important present, it was appreciated 100 percent and to demonstrate the fact that the one present became important, I kept the electric train for 57 years! The toy telephone that also served as a bank that I got for my fifth Christmas is still with me 60 years later!

Ask your kid or any kid on the block what they got for last Christmas and where it is today, less than a year later. Most presents are gone, trashed, discarded, and forgotten within months. Parents (and grandparents do this, also) give the kids presents to ease their conscience for neglecting the kid, for not spending quality time with him, for being at the job or the joint 95 percent of the kid's waking hours.

Did you ever hear of a "Slinky?" It's been around since 1945 and they are still selling them. It's a long spring coil. You place it on the top stair, the other end on the next step and it transfers the coils down the next step and next and so on until it gets down to the bottom of the stairs. A gift like this is cheap, lasts for years, and is educational. It is designed to capture the attention of a 5-year-old kid. Next Christmas, try a toy of this caliber. You probably have heard of the parents who spent several hundred dollars on a toy and about an hour after it was opened, they noticed that the kid was having a great time playing with the box it came in! Keep it simple! Don't overwhelm the kid with volumes of toys.

My son and his wife have a new kid and they have gotten this kid so many toys and stuffed animals that they are seriously considering buying a bigger house! Every room is full of toys and stuffed creatures. If the toy shelf ever tipped over, the stuffed bunnies, cats, dogs, and monkeys would certainly suffocate the kid. Do your kid a favor and give him your time, not gifts. They will be better off later in life.

As for computers, I do not consider them toys. Even though most can be used for games, they do teach computer skills. I have seen a kid 3 years old using the computer to play games. One big warning: They can get in trouble easily. Chat rooms or porn sites are available at the click of a mouse. Child molesters delight in using the Internet to snag a kid for their pleasure. If you hook them up to the Internet, be sure you monitor or block the X-rated sites unless you want to travel to a distant mall to retrieve your molested kid.

Sports

A good example of parents trying to relive their lives through their kids is obviously the "Tiger Woods" saga. The kid began swinging a club at 3 years old! Do you think a 3-year-old decided on his career at that age? Is a 3-year-old attracted to golf instead of playing in the sand with a toy truck? I doubt it. It appears to have worked out well, money-wise, for Woods and his father, but those thousands of hours spent on the golf course during his youth certainly deprived him of a normal teenager's life. Baseball, girls, dances, companionship of kids his age—these events can not be replaced by money. The famous A.J. Foyt did not encourage his son to enter auto racing. He told him, "Get an education." When at a later date, after the normal kid life and education was in place, he assisted him in entering the field. I would say this is the correct way to emphasize sports. Get the education and let the kid decide what he is going to do.

Little League is another area where parents tend to push their kids to excel. They want their bragging rights. "My kid had the game-winning homer last night and the Dismal Hollow Cubs beat the Big Flats Yankees." Parents have become so obsessed with Little League baseball and Pop Warner football that there have been many instances where parents have actually attacked the coaches for not using their kid in a game! Sports is a game, not a war. If you were a second stringer on the football team when you were in college, don't push the kid into football. He has heard enough of your stories about how you could have, should have. Let him make up his own mind and maybe you can brag about him leading the chess team to victory!

Most sports are good body-building efforts, but some dangers may be present. This may deter some kids from following in their father's footsteps. Auto racing is an example of families following in the same sport. Ned Jerret's a NASCAR champion who retired and became an announcer. He had the privilege of announcing the Daytona 500 when his son, Dale, won the event and Dale's son, Jason, is now a rookie on the same circuit. Tragedy can occur in that sport. Dale Ernhardt was killed in the 2001 Daytona 500, but his son, who finished second in that race, returned a week later to race again. The elder Ernhardt never pushed his kid into following in his footsteps, but after his son expressed interest and worked his way up through minor success, he hired him to drive one of his racers. Obviously, the kid was not being pushed by his father or he would have bowed out after the father's passing.

If your kid shows interest in any sport, even if it's not one of your favorites, I suggest helping him in that direction. He may become famous and buy you a new house, car, or prostitute to show his appreciation.

My uncle was severely injured driving a race car in the 1930s. It was never discussed by family members or among the children and until I decided on my own to pursue a career as a stock car racer in the 1960s, I never heard any family members discuss my uncle's racing. When I began building stock cars at my mother's home, the family immediately supported my choice. They told me later that they did not want to encourage any of the kids to get into the racing business due to the danger, and that's why they never discussed my uncle's career. Then they freely discussed the times that they had at the races, the events, and the friends they had made. Here was an example of a family that did its best to allow the offspring to pick the sports that he liked instead of just pushing him into the sport the family liked.

The best way for your kids to pick a sport is for him to try several, pick what he likes, and then go for it. Don't be a soccer mom/chauffeur. It's the kid's sport and if he really wants to play, he will find a way to get there and back. Tell him that you have a crowd phobia and can't ride in a minivan with 10 kids to games. If you want to watch, just appear in the stand at 8 p.m. with your mate or someone else. Have fun and enjoy the game!

Skooling

I know it's spelled wrong, I just wanted to check you out. Since my schooling was not extensive, I am not been a big believer in education that lasts nearly a third or even half of your productive years. Unless you are going to be a doctor or engineer and the education is a requirement to get a license, I would suggest aiming your kid at a practical goal.

If your kid appears to be a genius (and I would have someone else make the determination, since parents are inclined to declare the kid a genius if he can tie his shoes at 6 years old), you may want to encourage him to obtain a college degree or better. If your kid is average (and most are, that's how average is determined), high school may suffice.

Private schools are better than most public because their fellow students come from a better class of people. It may be worth sacrificing a little (e.g., don't buy dope this week) to get

the kid in with a good crowd. They may meet a classmate and even marry the person and a private school is a more likely place to find a kid who is destined to have a good profession or family money. If your kid marries into some cash, I'm sure it can ease your lifestyle later. It's a good investment.

My kids made a lot of friends in private school. If they had been in a public school, I'm sure it would have reduced their chances of being successful. Don't look for an easy school or convenient school. Look for a school that has produced winners in the past. It's not uncommon for a school to produce successful businessmen year after year. When I suggest not pushing kids into a profession or sport that you like, I do not mean to ignore them. Give a little guidance.

The high school I graduated from has a class reunion every five years. Being on the committee, I get to review the mailing list and I am always surprised at how many of these classmates did not become average factory Joe, 8-to-5 schmucks. More than 80 percent of my classmates owned their own business or were presidents of corporations. Most did this without benefit of further education than what they received at Edison Tech! I did not have assistance in deciding on my high school. I picked this school on my own and I am glad I did.

Some idiots decide that they are better teachers than the teacher and elect to "home school" the kids. There should be a law against this practice and I actually consider it child abuse. The morons who try to teach their kids at home deprive them of one of the greatest experiences in life, not to mention that these parents are stuck with their brats 24 hours a day! They deprive these kids of:

- The chance to make new acquaintances.
- The chance to mix socially with other kids their age and develop social skills.
- The chance to be part of a group, such as team sports.
- The chance of being exposed to a different environment, although they will be exposed to the bad (drug dealers and bullies) as well as the good, they will learn about the dangers.
- They will miss the chance to learn about the area, such as neighborhoods and bus routes that they would have been exposed to if they'd stayed home.
- They will not learn to respect the teacher.

As they say about a lawyer who defends himself that, "He has a fool for a client," The same applies to a parent who decides to teach his own kid: His kids have a fool for a teacher.

No parent is equipped to teach a kid from kindergarten through 12th grade. Even if you have a teaching degree, you are not qualified. A kid will probably have 25 subjects as he passes through the education system. Each of these teachers devotes his or her life to one particular subject. They are experts at that particular subject. If you are trying to replace that teacher and also do the cooking, cleaning, and laundry, you are a poor substitute.

Don't deprive your kids of a good education and a good social experience by trying to teach them yourself. One reason that you should be sure your kids get a good education is so they can support you in later life when your earning potential diminishes. It's like money in the bank! Get them a good education, if possible.

Pins and Needles

Pins and needles refer to piercing and tattoos. Every kid gets involved in fads, such as purple hair, baggy pants, and backward hats. These fads can be corrected at a later date by washing the dye out, getting bloomers that fit, or turning your hat around, but tattoos are pretty well permanent.

I have seen millions of tattoos and have never seen one that looks good. A study by a large college in New York recently sampled more than 6,000 kids ages 11-21 and found that 4.5 percent had tattoos. The study indicated that the kids with the tattoos were twice as likely to have had sexual intercourse and three times as likely to have smoked marijuana in the last month. They also lead the pack in other risk factors such as:

	Tattooed	Non-Tattooed
◆ Five or more drinks in a row in last year	78	45
◆ Smoked in last month	63	26
◆ Used marijuana in last month	38	12
◆ Had a serious fight in last year	54	32
◆ Inflicted injuries requiring medical care in last year	38	17
◆ Joined a gang in last year	14	4
◆ Ever truant from school	60	26
◆ Grade of "D" or less on last report card	52	29

Kids with tattoos are more likely than their peers to have parents with lower levels of education and to be from single-parent families. Many have tattoos or get tattooed to show their rebellion against society. That's OK when you are 16 or 17, but tattoos are forever. The kid will be rejected by most

employers unless he is looking for a job as a bouncer for a bar or wants to join the professional wrestlers. A tattoo will be a lifetime handicap. If you ever have been to Daytona for bike week, you may see the largest collection of tattooed people in the world. I have seen tattoos on every area of the body—penis, tongue, face, and ass—and although other needle freaks admired their artwork, the tattoos severely limited these bikers to mostly non-professional jobs.

The world is a cruel place and jobs don't come easy. Don't let your kid add an obstacle to his employment by getting an ink stain on his skin. A tattoo also may be a sign of other problems. If your kid insists on getting a tattoo, I would check to see if the kid has ever gravitated (floated freely in the air) in the past, if he has the numbers 666 anywhere on his head, or if his head has ever rotated 360 degrees. If any of these signs are or have been present, you should immediately contact the local priest.

Most kids want a tattoo because their friends have one. If they have friends who are of the tattoo type, you should chase

these friends away! Keep your kids away from the tattoo types and they may find more normal, socially acceptable friends. The previous chart should give you some indication of the lifestyles of the tattooed types.

Piercing is also an obnoxious sport. Why anyone would want a ring through his nose or lip or tongue or vital sex parts is beyond me, but it's done. This self-mutilation is not as bad as the tattoo because it may be rectified by simply removing the ring and it's over. There is however, extreme danger in poking holes through your body and infection can be a killer!

I would suggest that when the subject of self-mutilation comes up, you put your foot down (or in their posterior) and do not relent even when they say they will be the only one in the 6th grade without a tattoo or nose ring. Explain that kids want to self-mutilate so that they will appear "different." If your kid is the only one without the ink or rings, they will be the "different" one.

Age of Infinite Wisdom

All kids reach the age of infinite wisdom. For most it occurs at about the age of 16, 17, or 18. They have now learned all there is to know about sex, money, math, driving, housecleaning, sex, gardening, cleaning, dressing, investing, sex, law, geography, history, travel, religion, sex, employment, responsibility, sex, government, fashion, the military, drinking, drugs, sex, and sex! To put it another way, they know everything about everything (and sex) and there is absolutely nothing that you can say that they will listen to because they now have reached the age of infinite wisdom! What can you do? After years of study, I have concluded that there is only one answer to this question … nothing. Just stop any type of conversation with them for about a year. The age of infinite wisdom passes in about a year.

Monogrammed Shirts

Monogrammed means your name is on the pocket, front, or back. Many police agencies and missing children's groups recommend you never monogram your kid's moniker on his or her clothing. When child molesters or kidnappers are on the prowl, they look for kids with their names in plain sight. This gives them an in with the kid.

They walk up and address the kid by name, "Bobby, your father sent me over to pick you up because he is busy." Child molesters and kidnappers never want a conspicuous pick up. They want the kid to go along with them in a quiet orderly fashion so no one notices. If the kid is going to be fighting, screaming, and kicking as he is put in the burlap sack or car trunk, it will gain attention. By using the kid's name, it may actually appear to be a legitimate pick up. So here is the deal. If the kid is being a pain in the ass and you want to make him

a target for Chester the Molester, get him a nice shirt with his name on the front in big, block letters.

If the kid is being a good guy and helping around the house, get him a T-shirt with Mickey Mouse on it instead of his name. Now that you know the reasoning behind the monograms, you can decide what clothing is proper for the mood you are in.

The Birds and the Bees

I'm sure this could be an entire book if I was to cover it in the usual way. I'm going to skip over the actual act because you must have figured it out if you have a kid. You hear a lot about the birds and the bees but to this day I have never figured it out. What does it have to do with sex? Do birds do it to bees? Do bees do it to bees? Do you need a robin and a wasp when you do it? Is there some similarity to birds and bees when a guy and girl do it? Do they make a nest or a hive? Is there a buzzing sound? Do wings flap? Does one or the other have to sit on an egg?

I learned all about sex when I was just 12 years old from an older woman (she was 13!) and I'm glad I did. It was more fun than playing baseball and it only took two players, not 18! There was no special equipment to buy (well, except for condoms). It was more fun than going to a football game and it cost nothing! I tried to excel at this sport as best I could over

the next 60 years and have found it fun each time. If something is fun, why should you delay the experiences from your kid? When I was driving race cars, it was considered dangerous and sex was considered a safe pastime. In the past few years, that notion has reversed. With the advent of AIDS and the improved safety of race cars, race tracks, and race tires, racing has become reasonably safe and sex is more dangerous! If your kids are going to play the sex game, I would definitely explain—and furnish if necessary—all the proper devices to reduce pregnancy and spread of the AIDS virus and other sexually transmitted diseases. I would also explain that gay sex may be the most hazardous.

Talking sex to your offspring is a hard job. Before beginning, I would ask them to explain what they know. (You may learn a thing or two!) Remember, the Internet has a very large selection of sex sites and these kids are on the computer a lot when you are not around. If they are missing some of the ingredients, you can then fill in the blanks. Kids expect to get different directions from their parents. Every father will tell his son, "Go to it! Grab whatever you can!" Every mother will tell him the opposite. Every father will tell his daughter, "Just say no." Every mother will tell her daughter, "Save it for your wedding night." This has gone on since the beginning of time and guess what ... the kids ignore both parents.

I would however, impress them with one important item: If you are drinking or drugged up, avoid sex. Too many people have woken up in the morning with a person of the opposite sex in bed with them and not remembered the night before. It's a strange feeling (so I have been told; my wife reads these books!) And can have disastrous results: AIDS or kids!

The Family Picnic

Do you want your kids to associate with their cousins? (Don't answer this if you live in Tennessee, Arkansas, or Louisiana.) If the kids are part of a large family and the family gets together from time to time to share a keg or two and fry up a possum, your kid will come in contact with their first, second, and third cousins. Do these family members possess any bad habits that you don't want your kids to pick up?

They say you can pick your friends (and your kids' friends) but you can't pick your relatives. This saying was developed because of "funny uncles," weird kids, and other unusual family members. You don't want to expose the kids to any family members that may teach them bad habits.

If you do decide to go, be careful. You usually have no idea of the actual lifestyles of the picnic participants. You do not have any idea of their health problems that these people may

have, ranging from minor contagious diseases that may send you to the crapper for long visits, to something that could send you to the crypt.

If you don't know who prepares the porridge, don't eat it! These picnic participants may live in an environment that the humane society would object to. Just because you wash you hands every week or so, does not mean that your extended family does. The environments that you place your kids in has a lot to do with how they turn out. If your brother has three kids on dope at the family picnic and your sister has two girls that have matured to the point that the funny uncle is paying "special" attention to them, it may not be a good idea to expose your kids to the family flock.

TV Advertising Kids

Did you ever wonder how these fads like Beanie Babies catch on? It's not accidental. It's the result of about $12 billion annually being spent to pitch products to kids. It may be tied to a movie and cosponsored by a fast-food joint. It may be product placement in a kid's cartoon or advertising on a TV program designed for kids and it may also encourage violence. Do you want your kid to blow up a building or your house? Do you want them to take your AK-47 to school for target practice on live targets? Probably not.

To prevent the advertisers from grabbing your kid's brain, you must monitor what is on the tube. Children today on average spend 35 hours a week watching television, using the Internet and playing video games. What advertisers want is for children to buy, not to think. You can regulate what the kids see by not having TVs in their rooms and checking on what movies they are going to. If the movie is advertised as having a hundred killings, mutilations, and some sex, it may not be appropriate for kids. Use your head first and put your foot down second.

Eating Out

Many parents think it's nice to take their 5-year-old to a fancy restaurant. (I did once!) It is stupid as I found out in Niagra Falls, Canada, when my 5-year-old ate his French fries and pushed his steak away at Frank's Steak House. I could have taken the kid to the Golden Arches about 30 times for the price of the meal at Frank's gourmet restaurant!

If you have to take the kid out with you for grub, make it simple (also cheap). A kid will have a better time at the burger joint anytime. If you are an idiot (I was once!) and take them to a nice sit-down, romantic restaurant, the kid will hate it and the other patrons will hate you. Can you imagine your first date with Mr. Right or Ms. Right and you are sitting next to a kid rubbing mashed potatoes in his hair?!

Fancy restaurants are for fancy people. Kids are not fancy people. Leave them home, get a babysitter, and go yourself. Get a doggy bag and take the scraps home to the kids. They will love their meal.

D.I.V.O.R.C.E.

If the type on this chapter seems a little darker than the other chapters, it's because my secretary just went through a messy divorce and when anything concerning divorce comes in front of her for typing, she types with her fists instead of her fingers!

I have been married for what seems to be about 100 years, so I do not speak from actual experience, but I have a lot of firsthand knowledge about the effect of divorce on kids. Many, many, many years ago when I was in grammar school, my class had 47 students. Of that number, 46 came from two-parent families. Today, the same class has 30 students and 50 percent are from single-parent families. Divorce today is as common as trading in your old car!

I'm not a crusader for staying in bad marriages to benefit the kids because being around two adults who do not like each other is worse than being with a single parent. My sug-

gestion when divorce occurs is for the two partners to fight it out, tooth and nail between themselves and not involve the kid. Do not attempt to poison the kid's mind against the other spouse.

Since he will be with one parent at a time, it is a good chance for that parent to suggest that the other is a bastard, cheat, scum, rotten, perverted, worthless, communist, moron, thief, criminal, child molester, assassin, retarded piece of crap. When he is picked up on Friday night and spends the weekend with the other parent, he will then hear the other parent is a bastard, cheat, scum, rotten, perverted, worthless, communist, moron, thief, criminal, child molester, assassin, retarded piece of crap. To say at the least, this will be a mind-boggling experience for a young kid.

When he is asked by a judge, counselor or playmate what his mother is like, he will say she is a bastard, cheat, scum, rotten, perverted, worthless, communist, moron, thief, criminal, child molester, assassin, retarded piece of crap. When asked about his father, he wills say he's a bastard, cheat, scum, rotten, perverted, worthless, communist, moron, thief, criminal, child molester, assassin, retarded piece of crap. His grape-sized brain has been programmed to give these responses.

The kid should not be used as a pawn in a divorce. A good example of using a kid as a pawn is my granddaughter. I was instrumental in getting my son an attorney and appeared with him in divorce court. My ex-daughter-in-law obviously resented this and, I assume, continually referred to me as "F-ing Andy" whenever she mentioned my name. The 2-year-old kid picked up on this and whenever my son had the kid and came to visit us, the kid would ask, "where's F-ing Andy?"

To keep the kids out of the line of fire, I would suggest referring to the other spouse by his or her given name when the kid is around. Don't refer to the other spouse as the whore, scum, ass-wipe, even though you think it. The little rug rat did not have anything to do with your marital problems. If you screw up this kid's mind by involving him in the divorce, you will probably pay for it later in bail money, psychiatric help, or legal fees. Fight all you want with the ex, but the kid does not belong in this deal.

Grandpa, Grandma

Your mother and father from Kansas have called to inform you that they will be coming to visit for three weeks between the planting season and the weeding season this summer. What do you do? Rejoice! You and your spouse can also make plans since you know they will love to take care of the kids. You can be free! Plan for some romantic getaways (approximately three weeks' worth!). You should be there to greet them for an hour or so and be back before they leave.

If there are any odd jobs to be done around the house, obtain all the necessary paint, nails, wood, and cement and leave it in a conspicuous place. In the living room is a good spot to stockpile this material. Leave appropriate tools for grandpa because he may not bring his on "vacation."

These are the same people who brought up you or your mate. Did they do a good job? Are they qualified to give you

advice on bringing up kids? Keep in mind that their last experience at kid raising was 30 or 40 years ago. Things change. Knickers have gone out of style. Hair tonic is rare today. Although leisure suits looked good in the 1960s, they may not today. Penny loafers, bobby sox, and hoop skirts are long gone. What I'm getting at is the advice from grandma and grandpa should be ignored. It's out of date, but you can't just say, "bull——!" If they are offended, they may go to Florida next year instead of coming to your house for their vacation. Most of all, they may not buy the kids bicycles, clothes, toys, and stock. And if they don't, that means you will have to cover these items. That's expensive. So when they make a suggestion about what you are doing wrong, just say, "Thank you, I'll give that a try" or "I never would have thought of that. You're a great mom" and then forget about it as soon as they leave.

Be sure that when grandpa and grandma arrive, the freezer is full of frozen pizza or other kid delights. You may also get a bunch of gift certificates from all the fast food joints in the area and leave them with the grandfolks.

Do not give the grandparents your phone numbers for

emergencies. Tell them you are camping and the nearest phone is in a bar five miles away. If you give them a number, they may find a way to leave before the three weeks are up. You don't want them to sneak out the first time your 12-year-old comes home stoned. You should also be sure your liquor cabinet is securely locked to keep gramps on his good behavior.

Leaving the Nest

When my daughter was 18 years old, she left to be on her own. Not the day after she was 18, the same day. Either she could not stand us anymore or we were successful as parents and she had been instilled with all the information she needed to be on her own. I've never been sure which was the case. She never returned, even after her divorce.

Now, next was my son. He left, returned, left, returned, left, and returned from the time he was 18 until he was about 25. Sometimes he even returned with his latest fling. Each time he returned meant more laundry, beer, food, utilities, being awakened at 3 a.m. by a drunk, and use of our vehicles. I even got a call one night that my car was being impounded by the police in a distant city because the occupants were patronizing a prostitute! Needless to say, we were not happy to see him return to the nest so many times. Once, he even

took a job in Texas, a thousand miles away. We were happy, then he came back!

What should you do? Just have girls. Change your locks when they move and rent their rooms out as soon as they leave!

If you can, sell the abode and move to a distant location. Don't leave a forwarding address. Pretend you are in the Federal Witness Protection program, get a new identity, destroy your old credit cards, use a new name. When the bird kicks his offspring out of the nest, either they fly or thud. It works well for them.

Manners

I believe that teaching a kid manners is one of the most important things you can do. Even if he is stupid, going through life will be much easier with manners. In my line of work, I use "casual labor" frequently. "Casual labor" is a nice name for using misfits and morons for the dirtiest jobs on earth. Cleaning basements, scraping paint, and removing asbestos, are a few of the jobs these creatures do. Often I am surprised that one or two of these people actually have manners. They say thank you, please, excuse me, and use napkins to wipe the mustard off their chins. Although these people all get the same sweatshop pay and are about the same mentality, I automatically give the best of the jobs to the polite ones out of respect.

My grandkids all show great respect for adults. They don't interrupt adult conversations.

If your kids interrupt your conversation to request something for themselves, politely tell them to shut up the first time. If they do it a second time, refer to the chapter on punishment.

Grief Counselors

Did you ever notice that kids today are softer than 30 years ago? They are babied to every extent. If someone walks into the school yard and pops a couple of students, the next morning there are grief counselors throughout the school to assist the wimpy kids to cope with the loss of their classmates. I believe this coddling of the students encourages them to expect counseling any time any event disturbs their attitude. Pretty soon they will be calling in grief counselors if the basketball team loses an important game.

At one of the schools I attended, a fellow classmate was killed. They gave us a math test instead of counseling us. The test was, "There were 47 students in a class, one got killed. How many are left?"

We are overly protecting our kids and it will not help them in later life. Let them face reality. They will be better off for it.

Kids Do the Strangest Things

I'm sure by this time, you have realized that kids are prone to doing some strange things. One of my previous residences was a huge, three-story high mansion with an even higher peak to the roof. From the peak of the roof you could see yesterday and tomorrow! I sold this mansion to some friends, Chuck and Jean. Chuck had a teenage son and one night they found him on the peak of the roof and had to call the fire department to retrieve him!

Don't be surprised at anything your kid does. They have different brains than we do and it is impossible to anticipate what they may do. It usually has absolutely nothing to do with their parental training or genes. I don't believe anything Chuck ever did led to his son's escape to the roof. These kids can't be controlled or their actions anticipated.

Most times the best you can do is eliminate temptations. Don't leave the keys to your souped-up car or motorcycle lying around. Drink your booze as soon as you bring it home. Lock the workshop so they can't mutilate any of their pets on the bandsaw.

Things will still happen and your kid will not be the first to make or explode a bomb, derail a train, demolish the garage, set fire to his bedroom, or turn on a false alarm. When the unusual event does occur, keep in mind that there was nothing you could do to stop it and it's not your fault. Give them appropriate punishment and move on with your life.

Drive-Through Kid Disposal

The Golden Arches have had drive-throughs since the 1950s. There are drive-through beer and liquor stores, drive-through pharmacies, drive-through marriage chapels and drive-through tax preparers. It was just a matter of time until someone invented drive-through kid disposal sites.

New York and some other states have now adopted a law that allows for dropping off unwanted kids at police stations, libraries (I think you use the overdue-book box), fire houses, and post offices (postage may be required). This new law was to prevent unhappy parents from tossing kids in the Dumpster at the 7-11. Disposing of kids in Dumpsters is illegal and parents can be charged. (I'm not sure if they were charged with unauthorized dumping or child abuse.)

I have not been able to find out if there is an age limit to dropping off kids. Would it just be for newborns or could you drop off your 16-year-old when he became unmanageable? I believe this is a good law and being ecology minded, it will reduce the load on our landfills. I believe every parent should get a copy of this law and post it on the refrigerator as a warning to the kiddies.

Helpful Drugs

I believe that throughout history, there have only been three great drugs invented:

- Viagra
- Birth control pills
- Ritalin

The first two may not help with raising kids, but Ritalin works wonders. Ritalin is used to treat brats with attention deficit hyperactivity disorder (ADHD) and attention deficit disorder (ADD).

My limited research has indicated that all kids—yes, all, every one—have this disorder. Ritalin is intended to help the kid stay focused and concentrate, and to decrease the amount of uncontrolled behavior. Before this was invented, many parents had other methods of controlling kids. One was using a gas oven with the pilot light off and the other involved the tail pipe of a car. Believe me, Ritalin is much easier to use and less dangerous than the oven method of sedation.

Some parents and sitters feel that a child on Ritalin is much easier to control and I certainly agree. It also makes life easier for the parents. It's not an expensive drug, but it must be prescribed by a doctor. Just mention to your doctor that you have a kid and he will immediately prescribe the drug!

Money

I am a landlord and if I do not collect my rents when they are due, the day and hour they are due, most tenants would go out and spend it on dope, booze, or women. I must remember every date that rent is due. If I forget, the money will be gone forever.

To teach my kids that there are priorities in collecting their allowance at a predetermined time each week, I set up a schedule for getting their allowance. They had to ask me for the money on Saturday morning between 10 a.m. and noon. If they forgot, no allowance! This taught them some financial responsibility.

Another money problem will be that kids think it grows on trees. They want every new fad toy, game, or video. To keep them from knowing how much money you have, never discuss windfalls or bank balances in their presence. They can smell money and if they do, they will want you to spend it on them. Let the groceries run down and when you feed them bread (stale, if possible) and water for a couple of meals a month, mention that "things are hard right now, we've got lots of bills that need paying."

Give them the idea that poverty is just around the corner. This may reduce some of their demands for goodies. If you buy a new car, tell them that it's a "company car." If you and your mate are going on vacation, tell the kids it's a business trip. Treat your kids like mushrooms. Keep them in the dark.